# ANIMAL ALPHABET
## From A to Z

By Barbara Shook Hazen

O9-BHK-550

Illustrated
by
Adele Werber

MERRIGOLD PRESS • NEW YORK

ISBN: 0-307-90965-4          MCMXCI

# A

**A** is for **Alligator** on a log.

**B**

Brown **Bear** begins with **B.**

C is for the **Calf** that moos.

**Donkey** that brays starts with **D**.

# E

**E** is for **Elephant** taking a bath.

# F

**F** is for **Fox** on the forest path.

# G

**G** is for **Giraffe** that stands up tall.

**H** is for **Hippo**. He's biggest of all!

**I** is for **Ibis**
way up high.

**J** is for **Jaguar**
in the jungle wild.

# K

**K** is for **Kangaroo** and her child.

# L

**Lion** and his family start with **L**.

**M**

**M** is for **Monkey**. He swings very well.

**N**

**N** is for **Nightingale** that sweetly sings.

# O

The wise old **Owl** with **O** begins.

# P

**Prancing Pony** starts with **P.**

# Q

**Q** is for **Quail**. There are three.

**R** is for **Raccoon** on a limb.

**S** is for **Skunk**, mother and son.

**T**

**T** is for **Tiger** with a whiskered chin.

**U** is for **Unicorn**
in a book.

The nimble **Vicuna** begins with **V.**

**W** is for **Wolf** with a hungry look.

# X is for Xenurus.
He curls in a ball.

**Y** is for **Yak** with long shaggy hair.

**Z is for Zebra** striped everywhere.